YOUR KNOWLEDGE HAS VALUE

- We will publish your bachelor's and master's thesis, essays and papers

- Your own eBook and book -
  sold worldwide in all relevant shops

- Earn money with each sale

Upload your text at www.GRIN.com
and publish for free

Bibliographic information published by the German National Library:

The German National Library lists this publication in the National Bibliography; detailed bibliographic data are available on the Internet at http://dnb.dnb.de .

This book is copyright material and must not be copied, reproduced, transferred, distributed, leased, licensed or publicly performed or used in any way except as specifically permitted in writing by the publishers, as allowed under the terms and conditions under which it was purchased or as strictly permitted by applicable copyright law. Any unauthorized distribution or use of this text may be a direct infringement of the author s and publisher s rights and those responsible may be liable in law accordingly.

Imprint:

Copyright © 2017 GRIN Verlag, Open Publishing GmbH
Print and binding: Books on Demand GmbH, Norderstedt Germany
ISBN: 9783668510692

This book at GRIN:

http://www.grin.com/en/e-book/373659/the-potential-of-network-dynamics-for-organizations

Felix Zappe

The potential of network dynamics for organizations

A critical assessment

GRIN Publishing

GRIN - Your knowledge has value

Since its foundation in 1998, GRIN has specialized in publishing academic texts by students, college teachers and other academics as e-book and printed book. The website www.grin.com is an ideal platform for presenting term papers, final papers, scientific essays, dissertations and specialist books.

Visit us on the internet:

http://www.grin.com/

http://www.facebook.com/grincom

http://www.twitter.com/grin_com

The Potential of Network Dynamics for Organizations

Critical assessment of the manner in which organizations can harness the potential of network dynamics

Assignment as part of assessment for the study unit
New Digital Technologies

Handed in by: **Felix Zappe**

Written at the Edward de Bono Institute

University of Malta

Msida, June 2017

Content

TABLES AND FIGURES 2

1 INTRODUCTION 3

2 BASIC PRINCIPLES OF NETWORK ECONOMICS 3

   2.1 Relationships 3

   2.2 Network based businesses 4

   2.3 Network dynamics 6

3 THE ROLE OF NEW DIGITAL TECHNOLOGY 9

   3.1 The dimensions of network dynamics 9

   3.2 The network paradox 11

4 CONCLUSION 13

REFERENCES 14

Tables and figures

FIGURE 1: NETWORK VS. OUTLET CATEGORIZATION OF BUSINESSES (SOURCE: COYNE AND DYE, 1998). 5

FIGURE 2: PATTERNS OF NETWORK USAGE (SOURCE: COYNE AND DYE, 1998). 6

FIGURE 3: NETWORK EVOLUTION AND TECHNOLOGICAL CHANGE (SOURCE: CHOU AND ZOLKIEWSKI, 2012, P. 250). 9

TABLE 1: TECHNOLOGY'S ROLE IN HARNESSING NETWORK DYNAMICS (SOURCE: OWN DEPICTION) ... 10

TABLE 2: NETWORK PARADOX AND TECHNOLOGIES ROLE (SOURCE: OWN DEPICTION). 11

1 Introduction

The growing importance of networks can be seen in our everyday life. No day passes by without utilizing networks such as Facebook, LinkedIn, YouTube or even the information network Google. This network invasion shows the importance for the understanding of network dynamics and the importance for business to react accordingly to these new expectations and possibilities these technologies open up.

This work wants to introduce to basic principles of networking and then shortly assesses technologies possibilities in emerging frameworks.

2 Basic principles of network economics

This part of the work introduces into network economics by laying it its principles especially regarding relationships, then putting emphasize on network based business patterns and finally exploring network dynamics and their influence on the organization.

2.1 Relationships

Håkansson and Ford (2002) put the basic description of a network this way: In its most general appearance, a network is a construct of nodes that are related to each other, these specific relations are called threads. A market can be seen as a network where the nodes are businesses (i.e. the partakers of the market) and the ways in which they contribute to the market, i.e. their relationships between each other them are called threads. Threads and nodes in this context have their particular content each, as both are loaded with resources, knowledge and understanding in many different forms resulting from complex interactions, adaptations and investments within contributors of the network over time (ibid., p. 133).

Basically each business or network partaker is connected to each other contributor in the network by its unique technical and human resources. Singularly processed and from other actions isolated transactions are not happening in a network thus they shall be seen in their broader context of described complex long-term relationships. These relationships are ever changing to an extent where previous actions within said relationships are influencing the shape of future relationships. By that companies are enabled to deal with a rise of technological dependence and an increasing on the others needs for tailored offerings and more specific requirements (ibid., pp. 133-134).

Thus the relationships determine which businesses become parts of the network and how they are internally structured. But these relationships are also influencing each other. If three companies are connected by two business interactions each, any of these will depend on the third company's actions. The introduction of any resources or activities into a relationship will have either a positive or a negative influence on said relationship and also on the other relationships of the introducing party. A relationship thereby is defined by what has happened in the past in that relationship; what was previously learned by the parties; what does happen currently in this relationship and others; what are they expecting out of the relationship and the happenings in their indirect relationships. An interaction is always part of a relationship which in turn is always part of a wider network that needs to be understood. Thus the cost and benefits of a company's interaction are always determined by the relationship and the wider network it is part of (ibid., pp. 134).

Finally Håkansson and Ford (2002, p. 134) offer three major managerial questions about relationships that shall be asked before engaging in a relationship:

- What kind of special opportunities and restrictions does a network bring to a company?
- What is the interplay between influencing others and being influenced by them?
- How can a company control a network and what are the effects on the network and on the company?

2.2 Network based businesses

Despite the appearance of the relationships within the network, Coyne and Dye (1998) define the actual business model as an important part of the economics of networks. This business is summarized by the transport effect, i.e. the customer's value of the links in a network a company can provide.

So they define network-based businesses as those that deliver a significant portion of their value to their customers by transporting people, goods, or information from an entry point on a network to an exit point. These businesses can be categorized by the level degree to which their value to customers is caused by the network or in the individual outlets (see figure 1). This spectrum begins with the weakest network businesses on the far left, where most of the value to customers arises from the outlets. Moving to the right, an increasing proportion of value to the customer arises from the links between the outlets. Businesses at the far right operate almost entirely through networks (ibid.).

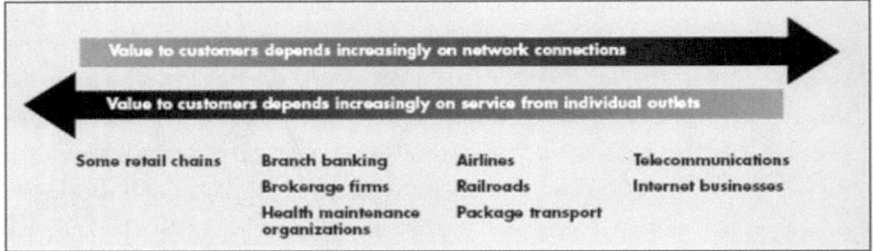

Figure 1: Network vs. Outlet categorization of businesses (Source: Coyne and Dye, 1998).

Further Coyne and Dye (ibid.) tracked customers' network usage patterns and found out that a given network can have different usage patterns depending on its customers. Managers usually assumed that customers used networks in the same way, meaning zero concentration. But in many networks, most customers concentrate their usage in separate zones, rarely using links to outlets outside those zones. In both zero-concentration and zone-concentration networks, some customers may heavily use links between certain outlets (see figure 2). For each pattern, companies need to follow a different strategy (ibid.):

- **Zero concentration:** customers use a network truly at random valuing the general connectivity of the entire network. Zero concentration is easy to recognize as no concentration emerges when link usage is mapped. Market share is related to the scale of the network, but not linear as adding an outlet will only slowly increase market share. But when the number of links exceeds that of most other competitors, share will rise sharply. Companies gain competitive advantage from differences in coverage and the first player to build a large network will usually a lasting front position, however it is difficult to stop expansion
- **Zone concentration:** In many networks, large numbers of customers concentrate their usage in some portions. Customers in a given area tend to concentrate their use of e.g. bank branches and ATMs according to a common pattern, these patterns form distinct zones. As some customers will always cross zone lines, these zones rarely have clear boundaries but maybe strategically separable. It is a main challenge to optimize the

trade-off between efficiency and effectiveness, involving the decision how many outlets to set up within a zone.

- **Lane concentration:** Customers heavily use or heavily value individual links in a network. Competition in that pattern tends to appear whenever a concentration of individual links is high enough to justify a dedicated system to serve them. A strategy to harvest this pattern might be to carry only the most profitable links and outlets so on does not need to subsidize the less profitable ones. New entrants often enjoy the potential of much lower labor costs. These advantages are facing disadvantages as obvious lack of the economies of scale and scope and the need to convince customers to accept multiple vendors i.e. managing a more complicated information flow. And thus influencing the key trade-off from the customers' perspective. Broad-network players can also offer bundled pricing to fend off a lane player's advances. Companies that provide the full range of package-shipping services, for example, can discount prices based on total customer shipments instead of pricing each package separately. Customers who chose separate lane providers would then jeopardize their overall price discounts. .For their part, lane competitors can work to decrease the complexity of their option for the customer.

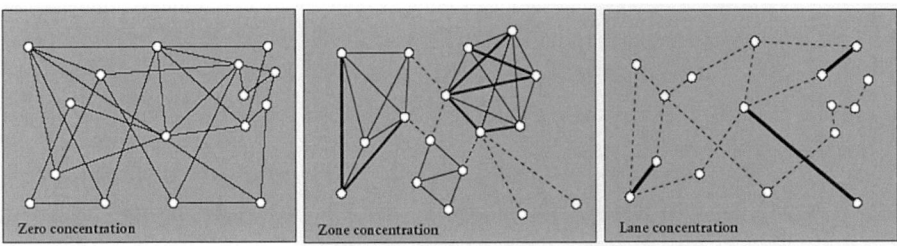

Figure 2: Patterns of network usage (Source: Coyne and Dye, 1998).

2.3 Network dynamics

Jabłoński (2015, p. 2) makes the assumption, that a network is dynamic, i.e. changes constantly, e.g. by only one participant in the network who can force changes through his or her actions in the whole network at any given situation. This mostly increases network effectiveness, which is defined as the attainment of positive network level outcomes that could not normally be achieved by individual organizational participants acting independently (Provan and Kenis, 2008). The function of the effectiveness accelerator is often played by a network coordinator, triggers and manages the activities of network members thus leading to the effect of dynamics in the network. The coordinator aims to achieve the expected effectiveness of value creation from the network and to manage the effectiveness of the division of value created from the relationship in the network (Jabłoński, 2015, p. 3).

These network dynamics underlie certain hypothesis formulated by Powell and White (2005):

- Accumulative advantage: Network expansion occurs through a process in which the most-connected nodes receive a disproportionate share of new thread
- Homophily: Network expansion follows a process in which new partners are chosen on the basis of their similarity to previous partners
- Follow-the=Trend: Network expansion entails herd like behavior, with participants matching their choices with the dominant choices of others, either in mutual response to common pressures from outside or through imitative behavior
- Multiconnectivity: Network expansion reflects a choice of partners that connect to one another through multiple independent paths, which increases reachability and the diversity of actors that are reachable.

In an attempt of putting these hypotheses into the broader perspective of system dynamics, Polowczyk (2012, as translated by Jabłoński, 2015, pp. 4-5) provides the basic principles of system dynamics as the following:

- The behavior of the system is endogenous, i.e. it results primarily from its internal structure (the microstructure determines macro-behavior)
- The fundamental element of the system structure is feedback. There are two types of feedback: positive and negative
- Positive feedback destabilizes the system. It reinforces upward or downward trends.
- Negative feedback brings stability as it offsets the effect of positive feedback and gives variables fluctuations in a sinus shaped pattern
- The behavior of systems is non-linear, which results from delays in reactions and the so-called sensitivity thresholds among them
- Different systems may have a similar structure (isomorphism).

- Systems of similar structure behave similar, have likewise dynamics and similar patterns of behavior.
- Decisions are made in the conditions of the limited rationality
- Used sources of information are: intuition (experience of experts), scientific theories and figures.
- The complexity of systems makes it hard to predict their behavior as they are counter-intuitive.

To deal with this high amount of complexity Lozano Platonoff (2009, as translated by Jabłoński, 2015, p. 5) introduces the approach of dynamic management, as basically "… an integrated process based on the collections of synthetic knowledge of the company and its environment, and how to continually update and improve it, enabling decision-makers to orient the company at meeting the short-term, medium-term and long-term expectations of the stakeholders in the best way possible." This approach features several characteristics such as (ibid.):

- Collections of synthetic knowledge about the company and its environment.
- The method of continuous updating of knowledge.
- The method of continuous improvement of knowledge.
- The integrated process that allows decision-makers to give direction to the company on a regular basis.
- Meeting short-, medium- and long-term expectations of stakeholders in the best way possible.

3 The role of new digital technology

The introduction of new digital technology and the associated change needs to be treated as an interactive process finally producing change forces that affect the ways of using or combining resources across a company's or a network's boundary and can only be understood from a processual point of view (Chou and Zolkiewski, 2012, p. 250). Thus technological change functions as the input and reflects an interactive process which can be seen as a transition period, while the reconfigured business or network is the output (ibid. see figure 3).

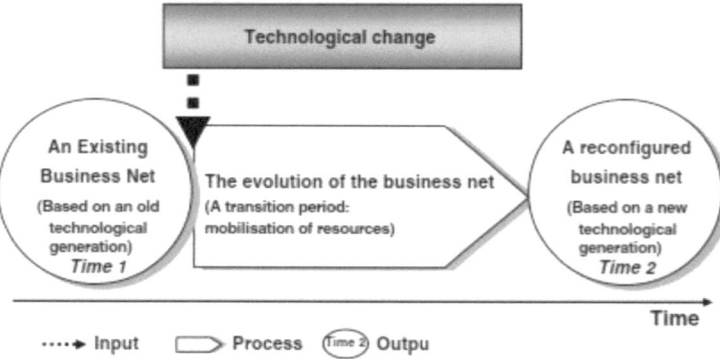

Figure 3: Network evolution and technological change (Source: Chou and Zolkiewski, 2012, p. 250).

This chapter assesses the possibilities of new digital technologies to deal with the challenges of network dynamics regarding their dimensions and their paradoxes.

3.1 The dimensions of network dynamics

In their paper Chou and Zolkiewski (2012) identify five dimensions of network dynamics, i.e. network boundary, time, process, events and positions / roles. Each of these dimensions can harness the potential of network dynamics, especially on an organizational level. For an assessment of these capabilities and the role of new digital technologies see table 1.

Table 1: Technology's role in harnessing network dynamics (Source: Own depiction).

Network dynamic dimension	Managerial implication (Chou and Zolkiewski, 2012, pp. 256-257)	Possible role of new digital technology
Network Boundaries	<ul><li>Foster co-creation especially through interfirm connections</li><li>Improve business relationships through respective network technology-bundles that forms an aggregate structure co-producing value for users</li></ul>	<ul><li>Establish a virtual meeting place with suppliers, customers and target customers to foster real co-creation</li><li>Foster exchange of experts no matter what company by social media</li><li>Use direct response tools such as survey apps or online live events to assess need, then advertise tech bundles at given places</li></ul>
Process	<ul><li>Managers need to have their strategic actions be in line with changing conditions</li><li>Foster business interaction</li><li>Have realistic expectations for the future</li></ul>	<ul><li>Be aware of changing conditions by using a digital feed reader, that sorts out all relevant news</li><li>Use online business platforms such as LinkedIn</li><li>Use the extensive knowledge about the future from the internet, e.g. by asking experts or involved brand ambassadors about their opinions</li></ul>
Time	<ul><li>Learn from the past</li><li>Be aware of relations made in the past</li></ul>	<ul><li>Use a digital logbook to objectively (e.g. more than 1 person) describe events as they happen and make notes about everything that was involved in the situation</li></ul>
Event	<ul><li>Evaluate milestone events for opportunities or constraints</li><li>Engage in sense making and strategizing</li></ul>	<ul><li>Use a company app to catch an atmospheric picture at key events</li><li>Foster employee and customer contributions in strategic questions (e.g. by</li></ul>

		social media).
Position / Role	• Adjust routines & structures • mobilization of resources • be in line with the environment	• Introduce quarter yearly adjustment meetings on online platforms • Use dynamic planning tools such as doodle to manage meetings and facilities • Foster a paperless office by using interactive technology

3.2 The network paradox

Håkansson and Ford (2002) propose managerial implications about the three network paradoxes, which can also be solved by using digital technology (see table 2).

Table 2: Network paradox and technologies role (Source: Own depiction).

Network Paradox (Håkansson and Ford, 2002, pp. 134-138)	Managerial implication (ibid.)	Possible role of new digital technology
1: **Opportunities and limitations:** The development of the threads gives opportunities to both nodes, but the existence of the threads also imposes restrictions on them.	• Actions are important to the living of the network • Expectation management • Change has to be made in existing relationships • Relationships can be standardized	• Assess your network by digital communication and interaction tracking • Share all your digital applications with your network to make reconciliation easier • Prevent yourself from wandering of by objectively assessing yourself and others • Digitally standardize as much as possible
2: **Influencing and being influenced in a network:** A network is both a way to influence and to be influ-	• Strategize and interact with your network • Believe in and work	• Use digital tools for information assessment, meeting and meeting post processing. Share it easily with e.g. evernote.

enced. Both situations exist simultaneously.	for the relationship • See the companies and the relationships as part of the network • Interact self-consciously	• Virtually track all your encounters with the other part to be aware of their importance • Get feedback after an interaction • Use video technology to improve your interactions
3: **Controlling and being out of control in networks**: The total network structure is dependent on how all of the threads are related to each other.	• Analyze your network position • Strategy is done within your network	• Digital Tracking software, RFID-Chips, social networks, email correspondences all can be used to assess your network position • Simulate your strategy using online tools or at very least a simple excel forecast with all your network's business figures • Meet up with your network, digitally but physically as often as possible

4 Conclusion

The analyses in chapter three has shown, that a lot of the tips given by the experts Chou and Zolkiewski as well as Håkansson and Ford can be very well supported with digital technology.

However the conclusions for the network dynamics seem to be a little farfetched and as a consequence arbitrary in their technical solution. However using the digital state of the art, i.e. online fora, social media and digital communication should help to at least improve business processes and efforts. Better solutions might be a great subject of further investigations.

The technological assessment of the network dynamic paradox however shows clearly, that you really have to be self- and network-aware to use your business network to the fullest. Technology might help to track things, but taking this responsibility from the entrepreneur is likely not to happen, as a great feeling for relationships is needed to steer a network. However technology might not be the solution but a contributor to one, as it helps the managers to perform their task and focus on their feelings. It might also be a limitation as much of personal feeling gets lost in technology. This extent of help or limitation might be an interesting topic for a further investigation.

5 References

Chou, H.-H. and Zolkiewski, J., 2012. Decoding network dynamics. *Industrial Marketing Ma-*
    nagement, 41, pp. 247-258.

Coyne, K. and Dye, R., 1998. The Competitive Dynamics of Network-Based Businesses. *Har-*
    vard Business Review, [online] Available at: https://hbr.org/1998/01/the-competitive-dynamics-of-network-based-businesses [Accessed 14 June 2017].

Håkansson, H. and D. Ford, D., 2002. How should companies interact in business networks? *Journal of Business Research,* 55, pp. 133–139.

Jabłoński, A., 2015. Network dynamics and business model dynamics in improving a company's performance. *International Journal of Economics, Commerce and Management,* 3 (1).

Lozano Platonoff, A., 2009. *Zarządzanie dynamiczne, Nowe podejście do zarządzania przedsiębiorstwem*. Warszawa: Difin.

Polowczyk, J., 2012. *Zarządzanie strategiczne w przedsiębiorstwie w ujęciu behawioralnym.* Poznań: Wydawnictwo Uniwersytetu Ekonomicznego w Poznaniu.

Powell, W.W. and White, D.R., 2005. Network Dynamics and Field Evolution: The Growth of
    Interorganizational Collaboration in the Life Sciences. *American Journal of Sociology*, 110 (4), pp. 1132–1205.

Provan, K.G. and Kenis, P., 2008. Modes of Network Governance: Structure, Management, and Effectiveness. *Journal of Public Administration Research and Theory,* 18 (2), pp. 229-252.

YOUR KNOWLEDGE HAS VALUE

- We will publish your bachelor's and master's thesis, essays and papers

- Your own eBook and book - sold worldwide in all relevant shops

- Earn money with each sale

Upload your text at www.GRIN.com
and publish for free